To Camari,

It's such a gift to connect with souls
(just as passionate about the arts
and the world as I am. ♡
In heavy & sometimes dark times,
these are the acts of love, the acts
of community that keep us going!
Thank you for what you do in
the poetry sphere.

CONTORTIONIST TONGUE

always,

Dania

CONTORTIONIST TONGUE

poetry & prose by

Dania Ayah Alkhouli

MOON
TIDE PRESS

~ 2020 ~

Contortionist Tongue
© Copyright 2020 Dania Ayah Alkhouli

Editor-in-chief
Eric Morago

Associate Editors
José Enrique Medina & Natalie Del Toro

Editor Emeritus
Michael Miller

Marketing Director
Dania Ayah Alkhouli

Marketing Assistant
Ellen Webre

Proofreader
Jim Hoggatt

Front cover art
Dania Ayah Alkhouli

Author photo
Karim Alkhouli

Book design
Michael Wada

Moon Tide logo design
Abraham Gomez

Contortionist Tongue
is published by Moon Tide Press

Moon Tide Press #166
6745 Washington Ave., Whittier, CA 90601
www.moontidepress.com

FIRST EDITION

Printed in the United States of America

ISBN # 978-1-7339493-6-1

In loving memory of daddy,
who will forever live on in my words and my work.

Table of Contents

INANNA

BROKEN LOVE LETTER

HOME & HEALING

INANNA

Frankenstein

This is no self-fulfilling prophecy.
I simply decided to wear the labels
you've been so keen on branding me with.
Etching them on to my skin,
like carvings into a tree trunk.
A violation of my organic nature
so when in Rome,
I'll be your devil's advocate.
And as long as you keep underestimating me,
I'll keep surprising you.
But don't you dare riot
when I burn you with my flames.
You set me on fire.
You built this monster.
I am nothing more
than your brainchild, oh Frankenstein.

Chimera

I had that dream again,
the one where I am pregnant.
Mama listens while making peanut butter
and jelly sandwiches for my brothers.
I make my own—labneh.
She folds over the brown paper bag
with such symmetry and says,
Arab traditions believe dreams
of pregnancy mean you're carrying
a heavy burden.

Muslim. Syrian. American. Woman.
Four weights the world made
too heavy to carry.
Identities battling inside me.
Kicking, rolling, too many
pulsating heartbeats.
How do I birth them into one?

Science traditions believe mothers
spend eternity carrying
the DNA of their offspring
post birth—meaning they carry
the DNA of what they birthed,
with the DNA of what birthed them.
So, who do they ever become?

Labneh, I realize, after three bites,
in my loud high school cafeteria,
is not meant for square white bread
but rather the round full pita instead.
And I wonder, do boys ever have dreams
of being pregnant?

Nothing Wrong with You

He asks if I want something
to be wrong with me.
In Arabic, silence is agreeing;
I say nothing.

There is nothing wrong with you, he says.
I wonder what fuels this relief,
hearing a white man tell me so.

When a woman is this full, he continues,
this complete, she is an attraction.
The sun everyone basks in.
The static blue light of magnetic desire
they latently gravitate towards.
But after a while the depth morphs into heavy water
for them—
too much hydrogen and not enough oxygen.
An asphyxiation.
Cause of death:
Their subconscious choice not to swim.
So they drown;
pin the blame on her,
and call it leaving.

I did not ask to be the sun
or the heavy water.
The voluptuous cylinder of fire and ice
every mother warns her child about.
How do I extinguish my flames?
Chisel away points of icicles nicknamed rough edges?
Become a woman without the caution tape.
The DO NOT CROSS lines.
Amenable enough to fit inside white chalk outlines.
In palms of unworthy hands.
A woman finally the right amount
instead of the supernova—

beautiful only
in the catastrophe of her death.

Spanish Omelette

I tell him what I want to do with my body
over a plate of chips and salsa.
The words fall easily from my lips,
and he looks at me, gaze fixed
deep and says, *What do you mean
you don't want children? What's wrong with you?*

I have known my soul is not destined
for motherhood, even if my body is.
Nothing is wrong with me, I say.

A broken record starts spinning.
His voice, the vinyl scratching
like echoes within me, as if I were hollow.

I am not, but he looks as though being with me
is an exchange of empty nest for emptiness.
Like I were just a body, nothing more,
and a vacant one at that.

*Well if there's nothing physically wrong with you,
and are choosing to not have children,
there must be something mentally wrong with you.*

My tongue now tries to lick the ends
of his phrases; frayed strings of identities
I hope will become one thread for the needle
meant to weave femininity back into my female,
womanhood back into my womb.

God made man and man thinks he makes me.
Takes that needle and threads puppet strings
from my shoulders to the sky.
No wonder I walk hunched
over in shame, hiding all my curves.
Even the one deemed acceptable,
the one I do not have—the curve of a belly, full.

The server comes back to take an order.
I look down at the menu, away from all eyes—
appetite stolen just as quickly as the rights to my body
—and there I am, listed
on the left side of the menu, under BREAKFAST.
My eggs and I fluffed into nothing more
than ingredients for yet another man's plate.

thread count

when history glorifies our bodies
as sexual tapestries for men
to weave, why are we shamed
for loving our own threads?
how did the apotheosis of sexuality
become a right of men?
a threshold feminine feet cannot cross?

what a dare it is to thread the needle
with our own fingers, penetrate
and sew our own masterpieces.

for centuries the colors of our pleasures
have been painted by hands not our own.
our bodies, narrated;
built like hourglasses
to remind us of the countdown
every time we look in the mirror.
biological clocks violently ticking
like time bombs, activated
by the same hands that built us.

i dare my eyes to see my body,
and they find skin on skin,
reminding me of the parts of my womanhood
i was told to forget.
a journey to conquer the fronts of a body
once put to shame.
i graze curves,
feel a history never known to me,
a future i can touch.
a territory i get to rename,
and i wonder
what ever would a man taste like
now, having sunk fangs deep
into the flesh of loving myself?

wanted

I ask her   to help me   zip my dress.

Her palm finds   its way onto   my low back.

Catches other curves   of my body,   unseen. *Mashallah, girl*

your boobs, wow!   I laugh nervously   sucking in unwanted

curves to get   the zipper up.   *No, really, damn!*

I force myself   to look up   into the mirror.

I have finally   *found my body*   *and I'll never*

stop   *wearing*   *it.*

17

How to Cut a Woman

A woman's skin must be the most cutting-edge cutting board.
Thick nature to withstand everything on it, sliced.
Nothing standing between her and the blade.
She, the intended target of that wound to be made.
Thick nature to withstand everything on it, sliced.
From the fruits of her labor to the truths of her tongue.
She, the intended target of that wound to be made.
Lay her flat, and stroke the ridges of past cuts.
From the fruits of her labor to the truths of her tongue.
Some wounds stop bleeding but do not heal.
Lay her flat, and stroke the ridges of past cuts.
A story mapped out by the hands that hold the knife.
Some wounds stop bleeding but do not heal.
Triaged beneath what will come.
A story mapped out by the hands that hold the knife.
Are any of those hands hers?
Triaged beneath what will come.
Nothing standing between her and the blade.
Are any of those hands hers?
A woman's skin must be the most cutting edge.

Sisterhood

I told her the breakup
of friendships
always hurts more
than fraying ties with a man.
I'll never need a man.
I'll always need my sister.
She swore
upon our eternal sisterhood
—our love—
beneath a full moon
that smiled at us.
Said she never met anyone else
who too could see the moon's face.
But that's me, seeing things
left unseen.
Staying in places
unwelcome.
Like with people. Like in love.

I have always been able to see
the moon's face—seen right through it.
A mocking expression
staring back at me.
Illuminated only
by the light of another.
Incapable of glowing itself.
A reminder of the world around me—
stealing my light
to brighten their darkness,
and still asking how much more.

Sometimes the sun needs love too.
Sometimes love is *Thank You*.
Is leaving a note
before you go.
Explaining why
you want to go,
or at the very least
that you're going.

I always write goodbye notes,
even when it's the other person
who's leaving.

Unbelievers

I am becoming the ruins
Syria has become; ages
of forgotten worth further destroyed.
But this recognition does not save ~~me~~ us.
Taken for granted for so many years,
only God keeps count now.

We have become unbelievers
in the faith of being saved.
As forgotten as the status of Zenobia—
Queen of Palmyra.
What good are hands of a savior
when they too belong to an oppressor?
Both sides of the same coin have men
with hands that touch what was never theirs.

This is how I know Syria is a woman.
What other being could be as envied as she?
Proudly standing tall, on her own.
An independent woman
unknowingly seducing destruction
in the being of herself.
Bold. Loud. Red
lipstick in the face of the enemy.
Unyielding, unlike her neighbors.

No foreigner could keep her long—
she always found her way,
and that's what set off the grenade.
Those red lips forced to kiss
Red Lines everyone crossed with immunity.
Erasing footprints of centuries from her shoulders.

Are women anatomically made to hyperextend?
Expand our bodies in pain to shelter others?
Is this why we tire of giving birth?
Done with reproducing a child
who ends up becoming the next Oedipus.
Slaughtering mothers before fathers because
Women are speaking for themselves.

Shame on humanity for trying to silence
the mother of language.
Pretending the alphabets on our tongues,
the music in our ears,
the navigation beneath our fingers,
did not come from our Ugarit coasts—
merging generations like land and sea.

Shame on humanity for leaving us stranded.
For making us become unbelievers
in the faith of being saved.

I am tired.   We,

we are tired.

We,

Syria,   me.

We are tired. We,

Syrian   women.

We are tired. We,

women,   are tired.

Junkyard

She holds it with a hand.
Inspectingly, bewildered.
It's broken, she says,
so matter of factly.
Like it were material—
a toaster or radio.
Disposable, replaceable.

Confirming my thoughts she says,
You're not heartbroken;
your heart is broken.
An emphasis on the differentiation.
As in my heart is a car, totaled.
A wreckage unsalvageable.
Metal twisted so tightly
it's become a set of braids
mortal hands can never untangle.

Backseat

In my 30 years of flying, I never once reclined my seat back—not even an inch. If that tells you anything about me let it be that I've spent my entire life ensuring everyone else's comfort at the expense of mine. And maybe that's why I have always lived a very difficult life. Maybe that's why I *still* live a very difficult life. Incapable of stripping away decades of training on how to be a woman. A daughter of immigrants. A believer in God. A passenger in the backseat.

Walking on so many eggshells I learned to construct mosaic portraits to hang on the walls of every house of God I tried to find refuge in. I get why they call it a *house* of worship. They never built it to feel like a home. Soaking anxiety in scripture doesn't make it go away. Lighting a candle for depression does not smoke out the demons, especially if they're real (people).

Last year I made my first resolution. Told my mom I wanted to become a bitch. Bitches have best friends. Bitches have men staying. Bitches have it all. She said I was too good to become a bitch but by the end of the year, I had mastered the art of bitch-hood. Broken enough by two loves, my born-again demons found their way home.

The world still didn't welcome me. I realized it was neither the saint in me nor the sinner that the world didn't like, it was just me.

The tempting thing about suicide is that you yourself won't have to deal with the aftermath. The aftermath that leaves you painfully overthinking, *What will happen to…? What will be of…?*

I won't be left behind to clean up the mess, which would ironically be the first time I am not left behind and the first time I am not the one cleaning up the mess. But deep down I know I could never do it—suicide. I couldn't before, not even when it was one of the three choices I had: Stay and wait for the day when anger would get the better of him and death would actually do us part or suffer the repercussions of leaving a man in a patriarchal world.

Five years later and I still deal with the latter. Wondering if I should have stayed or if I should have left the world instead of the man. I didn't possess the courage (I still don't) and I don't know why we we're taught that suicide is an act of cowardice when it clearly requires the utmost strength.

My fingers trace over the jagged mosaic hangings. Salted caramel tears and cracked blood give color to my past and I pray, more than anything, to just once be able to recline my seat back, even if just an inch.

This Is How It Feels to Be a Woman

Ever watched a candle
extinguish
in a jar.
Lid carefully placed atop.
Suffocating to its last breath.
A flame losing its will to burn
against its will.

Done.

Permits

How do you let this destroy you?

Sometimes mothers
ask questions that make no sense.
Questions that have no answers.
I wonder if this is one
of the many reasons I choose
not to become one.
Fearing never being able
to ask the perfect questions
that have no answers.
Fearing a daughter
who does not answer.
But even more so fearing
a son who does.

I didn't *let* this destroy me.
It just did, without my consent.
I am not a concrete building.
Demolitions do not come to me
for permits before happening.
They just happen, and I am always left
alone beneath the rubble.
The man-made rubble.
Men know nothing
but destruction.
Women only know of construction.
But we tire of being
the only ones building
homes, love, men.
What joy it must be to cause a chaos
you do not have to quiet.
To make a mess you never have to clean.
To possess the freedom,
the privilege, to break things
at will, without reason, for game.
I've never seen little girls jump
in puddles or on piled up leaves,

but men know of foliage.
The crunching sounds of death
it makes beneath their feet.
Women know of its softness.
Its need to be swept away
gently, and here I am,
being asked another perfect question
by a woman, about why I didn't build
a stronger armor against man.
As if I am the one responsible
for man and his destructions.

Is that how I let this destroy me?

BROKEN LOVE LETTER

Original Sin

Believing in a good man
is like believing in God.
Unseen, yet existing.
Till you remember
God and man are unalike.
One is always there,
the other, never present.
Blessed be
the relationship
where I pray to
instead of for.
This codependence on Eve
~~was~~ *is* man's original sin.

Love Thy Enemies

When they say
Pray for those who hurt you,
they must be talking about those you hate
because I still can't get myself to pray
for the man I love.

Jiddo is Right

Love poems aren't real.
My grandfather tells me this
as he carefully clips an Arabic newspaper
for another scrapbook collection.

His final contributions to preserving
lessons from history. Pieces of culture
frozen in time, in hopes his grandchildren
will never forget,

even after he is gone.
I look at him in admiration and curiosity.
So classy and wise, even in his 90s.
Wearing a cotton striped robe de chambre,

square brown glasses, in the Damascene
living room of my childhood summers.
The afternoon sun illuminates through the balcony,
where sounds of men speaking Arabic

echo up from the streets.
Quite the contrast to the sounds of bombs
that shook our house the night before.
His statement comes across matter-of-fact,

like his granddaughter—the writer
who inherited his pen—
should have already known this.
But Jiddo, what about all the romantic love poems?

He does not look up but lifts a neon marker—
foreshadowing a highlight of the words to come,
both on and off paper.
Those are not words of love; because someone

truly in love, is incapable of capturing it.
When you are in love, you can never
put those feelings into tangible words.
I think of all the men of my past

poems, the ease of letting them go
on paper, when our final grains of sand fell.
Then I think of the only man who left me speechless,
who I could never immortalize in pages.

I smile, softly, nostalgia intertwining with epiphany.
Two pages of my story stuck together. Jiddo glues
the last clipping into the scrapbook and looks up at me.
We cave to the smell of malookhiyeh calling our bellies to lunch.

Another Way to Say I Love You

Baggage is nothing more
than something
we can unpack [together].

First Edition

How can I trust you when I don't even know you?
Sure, I know *of* you—the CliffsNotes version—
but I hunger for the unabridged texts of your story.
Thick pages of details and edits.
Lines crossed, erased, and rewritten.

But do I really want to be so well-versed in a man
who has yet to read me?
A man who tears out his own pages
in an attempt to become the mystery
novel he needn't be?

If only you could see past my cover.
Past the synopsis on my backside,
and deep beneath the skin, where my stories lie.
Such a shame we've sat beside each other for years,
on the dusty shelves of this orbiting library of our Milky Way.
Old sepia souls pressed between pages,
yearning to be read, delved into
like sacred scriptures worth memorizing.

What scares you about letting me crack
open your heavy cover?
Showing me words beyond the preface?
These hands are those of a writer,
so what better hands to cradle you than mine?
To hold you close. Turn your pages gently
but often, lavishing in your story.
I would repair your broken spine every time.
Never replace you with the newest release,
because you are the original—my signed first edition.
Aged, antique, vintage, and unique.

Let me read you, cover to cover,
in every language we know.
From English to Arabic to Spanish.
I want to nestle with you at the end of a long day.
Feel the texture of your worn-out pages,
the ridges of folded sheets,
and know you as the bedtime stories of our ancestors.

Building a Bookcase

Fingers stroke a naked wall;
softly draw unspoken measurements.
Make impressions, *deep.*
A foreshadowing
of what we've long hungered for.
A home to house our stories
in languages mastered
by bodies before tongues.
Skins touch, the lightest graze
with the heaviest intentions.
Feel raw flesh
to find the resting place
of rabbet joints; cut
sharp incisions
to make our parts fit.
Assemble the unit.
Stack hips,
affixing one atop the other, and grind
away rough edges
with sandpaper determination.
Slide shelves, wet
with glue, to hold weights
arms cannot—
one bone at a time.
Press firmly,
hold, then release.
Let dry, and finish
with a stain.

Catch 22

I never wanted to fix him.
I wanted to heal him,
but he loved being broken.
A jigsaw-puzzle
he never wanted
to put back together.
Edges so sharp he bled,
along with everyone else
who tried to love him.

how an arab actor dumps you

3:50 p.m.
arrive at the cafe.
his hug—
the greatest relief
as usual.

4:27 p.m.
over iced tea
and sparkling water
he tells you
he doesn't want this
anymore.
never did (in the first place).
tells you he feels regretful. guilty.
apologizes but says nothing
that tastes good.
finally he swallows silence.
bittersweet.

4:41 p.m.
tears stream.
only yours.
ask, *now what*?
he says, *now*
i walk you to your car
and say goodbye.

7:15 p.m.
google affordable therapy.
book an appointment
with a cost-effective therapist
from the internet.
a straight white man.
question why *him*.
stop questioning.
surrender to the past
two years.
claim defeat and wait

for hope.
you've been dying
to heal
but time
doesn't heal things
that weren't meant to be broken.

10:01 p.m.
your mom cries
as she holds
a sobbing daughter.
for the first time, losing a man
feels like losing something
that was meant to be yours.
that was already a part of you
then stolen.
he felt like home
and home is a transplant
rejected.
you haven't felt welcome
anywhere
in a long time
but your soul was engraved
on his arms,
and it didn't take too long
for them to call you.

1:15 a.m.
eyes burn from salt
and sleeplessness.
turn off the television.
dread sleep because the worst
part of this is waking up
and realizing it was no nightmare.
the wound on the left part
of your chest is real,
is excruciating.
his name will no longer grace
your screen.
no more good morning texts
that made waking up worthwhile
after a long time
of feeling otherwise.

2:26 a.m.
yelp dance classes.
question whether they would
be more beneficial
than traditional therapy.
after all,
dance comes second to poetry
and third to oxygen
for survival.
it's healed you every time
before and it's been a while
since you moved
for yourself
instead of a man.
your body starts to feel alive
at just the thought.
fantasize about dancing
with a man
who'll want to be your partner
for more than just two months.
more than just nine.
more than just eighteen.
for more than forever
for once.

3:07 a.m.
cry yourself (not) to sleep
as you clench at your heart
and pray,
this time around,
you don't wake up.

Kiss of Death

I call you
with only a touch
of our hands.

Telling you,
for old times' sake,
kiss me once more.
Kiss me and take
my breath away,
the life you exhaled
into me.

You tasted death
unfairly, and now
you're making me
eat it too.

Psychology of Seduction

The first time I met my inner seductress (because that sounds more kosher than "inner ho") I was 15 and in religious studies, of all places. My teacher, talking about extramarital sex—one of the big sins— ventured off into the ever so misogynistic rant about how the key to both locking and unlocking promiscuity, is in the hands of women because we are the temptresses. Therefore doomed to an eternity of extra responsibilities for this great power. Meaning, men, yet again, are off the hook from accountability.

We're told Eve ate from the forbidden tree then seduced her husband into it, when the original scriptures clarify they both bit into temptation. So how did we become the ever so dangerous, sexually ticking time bombs to be diffused? And when did it become against human nature for women themselves to be *human* and feel desire?

Nonetheless, the seductress surfaced. She was intrigued. Had never been acknowledged before, and now she was being given such a grandeur introduction she had to make an entrance. Take a bow. I booed her off stage. Told her she was the devilish part of me I would never want or need. Insert 13 years.

I read once that when a girl gets her heart broken, her ho status is activated. For years my heart felt the weight of every man's foot crush it on his way out, but apparently it never broke because nothing happened to me until I met *him*.

He broke my heart from the get-go and whenever I thought I let him go, I was only falling deeper. The inner seductress found her soul mate and that's not to say this makes us an unhealthy combustible excitingly addictive dynamic, but it is to say that this was probably what I've been waiting for my *entire* life. Ho status activated and I'm not ashamed. But I will say he better get his shit together and keep me, because he's never going to find a more phenomenal ho...*seductress*. The Lady and the tramp. The innocent-looking but forever guilty. The *can cook dinner and offer more than one dessert* ho. The *run an entire organization, recite a thousand poems, write a book, get a Master's degree, dance like a goddess, write another book, drive on the 110 Freeway at 5:37 p.m., and still have the energy for whatever he wants* seductress.

No man has ever made me feel so ridiculously powerful yet so ultimately weak at the same damn time, but I love every single bit of it. All the pain and all the pleasure because it outweighs the list of pros to leaving him. But sometimes he can't see that. He feels it when I wake up in his arms and we share coffee by that small window as he smokes his cigarette. But when I kiss him goodbye, I ache because our farewells have far too much distance in between them.

What is it with men and not committing to fucking amazing women? Is this that whole "run from what makes them feel too good" shit? Am I the only crazy soul who runs towards what makes me happy?

One year is too long when I walk out his door but not long enough when we're mid love. Time doesn't seem to stand still for us. It's always against the hos. Passing by, trying to fast forward through our sins to the supposedly coming better days of repentance but I swear, I've tasted nothing better than him.

Sin & Love

You made loving you
feel like sin
and now sinning
is the only love I know
how to show.

Work of Art

Men gravitate
towards the sins of me.
Magnets, called
in by heavy metals.
Unclean themselves
but compelled to cleanse me.
To break the energy
of my attraction
in everyone else.

Men, you are no gods.
Do not try and save me
from myself.
I worship what I am.
I need no salvation.
Goddesses do not entertain.
We exist.

Just look at every woman
in history books and museums.
Which one of them is smiling?
I do not want to be remembered
for the face I can make on demand
and don't.
I want to be remembered
for the demands I make
and execute.

I was always meant to be broken.
Jagged abstract art.
Priceless femininity and strength.
And a masterpiece
is not meant to be changed.
Is not meant to be in the arms of men
who have expensive tastes
they cannot afford.

Human // Nature

The forbidden fruit
did nothing more
than hang
from a tree.
It was man who
succumbed to his
weakness, plucked her
from where she belongs—
from home—
and spends his
lifetime cutting down
trees. Finding relief
in destruction. Yelling
timber at every fall

but his.

Bedroom Crusades

You learn how to swim quicker when you're thrust into the dark waters instead of being led in toe by toe, left to find the surface for yourself. However, you learn the darker ways of survival like this. You become an expert swimmer but with a sadistic vantage point. This is what the woman underneath you is comprised of.

A well-versed sexual artist, digging her nails into your back in a statement to refill the ink of her stories. Wearing newly exfoliated skin, born from the sands of her jagged history with abuse. I won't apologize for my nature to want you. To have you and all that we do, but shouldn't. Like anticipate the graze of our teeth against each other's bitter, sweet skin. Like gasp with every millimeter of depth we find ourselves capable of taking. I've never wanted someone like I want you and in the way that I want you—an addiction I refuse to withdraw from. A detrimental corruptive force I embrace like arms around a wrecking ball.

Wreck me.

I'm so tired of being so put together, so whole, so locked away. Wreck me. Shatter me to my core and make me scream. I give up on trying to get over you, I'm clearly only good at getting under you. So ride me, hard, and yet, gentle. Master this circus running wild through me. With your lips, as they discover the stunning wonders of my body. With your contortionist tongue, creating geometric patterns throughout its long marvelous strokes. Wildly, warmly, a wetness I can't resist. An acrobatic performance, diving into me with no safety net.

I love how I taste on you just as much as you love tasting me too, and only a clean woman with a dirty mind can say that, and you're in luck, because that's exactly what I am. I may not know every dirty word in the Urban Dictionary but I'm more of a hands-on learner. Lucky you, although a lucky man is only one who knows what it is that makes him lucky. Luck be a lady, and here I am tonight.

So conquer this world of me, then step aside and surrender your throne. As Queen I can show you everything and more when I slide on top of you. It's not only my tongue that can't tell lies. My hips have their fair share of truth they're ready to show. An exotic ancestry reinforced in their hypnotic width and motions as they ebb and flow over you. Watch me dance for you, then dance circles around you because it's not just my crown that I'm going to wear. You look good on me and, let's not kid ourselves, I look damn sexy on you too.

And what I want—when you ask me to whisper my greatest desires between those sheets—is to erase the mistake of you with another mistake of you. Keep the taste of you in my mouth for as long as you can last. Gently suck away the heavy sorrows of the day and become as weightless as the exhale you release. Climb my way up from your toes and down from your navel. Navigate the map of a man I thought I knew. Explore the jungles of your chest and thighs, savor your many peaks and flavors that make me want to bite you as often as I bite my own lip.

Because even when it hurts it feels like divinity. A christening pleasure to awaken the dead within us. We rise and fall with them as our skins become one in the warmth we create. The pulsation throbbing with such a force, such a melody, it becomes the soundtrack to our sex in these bedroom crusades.

Start out slow and take your time. Play with me and work like a ripple in reverse, moving to me from the outside in. Creating waves on the shores of our bodies. Move me to breathlessness and make me serenade you with sonnets superseding the iambic pentameter of the pulses escalating between my thighs. And when you finally get me right, when you've made me hotter and wetter than your eyes do on any given day, take me.

Take me from the front, from behind, from any and every angle that crosses your mind. Just take me, but then keep me, with your hands and that supposed skillful wisdom. Cradle and kiss every single one of my curves, sacredly. From my shoulders to my breasts to my waist, they call out for your touch longingly, every time you let go. A bitter farewell they tire of giving so don't keep your hands to yourself, and don't go easy on me either. I'm young, not weak.

The weight of your body pinned against mine keeps me grounded. An eager captive beneath the heavy fantasies I want you to share. Say everything to me and leave nothing on the tip of your tongue, except the strategic paths you'll take with it across my skin. Connecting the dots of my freckles to reveal every secret I will no longer keep.

Atlantis

Two types of tears drown you after sin:
Guilt over what you will never do again
or guilt over what you will never be able to stop doing.
I dare you to guess which of these two oceans
I've made an Atlantis for you.

Stain

I wish you lasted on my heart
as long as you lasted on my tongue.
Not even 24 hours before the taste
of your cigarette and wine-stained breath fades
from my lips, and I begin suffering the withdrawals.
Craving your flavor, your breath of life,
and no drink was ever more (bitter)sweet.

Nostalgic for Heartaches

You didn't break my heart,
you broke me,
and that is far worse
because my heart
is only a part of me.
I, am all of me.

Karma in a Bottle

If you want to use women
as temporary anesthetics to heal
those wounds of yours
you won't mend for yourself, then get creative.
Utilize a bit of that supposed intelligence—
that age-old wisdom—and diversify your tactics.
Don't fuck women who run
in the same circle. Women talk.
Eventually it'll all come out,
and I'll go ahead and tell you,
it's already out.
Your reputation precedes you
but I wanted to give you
the benefit of the doubt.
Hear it directly from the source.
To play a woman well
and throw her away
leaves her scorned, and rightfully so.
I won't destroy you with the truth,
because unlike them I fell
for you, after all this time.
But I will warn others—keep them safe.
I will write poems, sonnets of realism
to haunt you on your lonely nights.
At the bottom of those empty wine bottles
you'll wish to fill with messages of regret
and throw back at me.
No woman deserves to endure this shit
from you or from any man
incapable of securing himself.

I offered to lick your wounds clean
and instead you created wounds
of my own I now have to heal.
Maybe you can't see my blood
but that doesn't mean I'm not bleeding.
Didn't religion teach you to believe in the unseen?
So worship in my pain.
I do not need to shed before you
to be real.

L'homme

He spent hours making me
feel useless
and only minutes using me.

Love Poem
Inspired by a discussion with A.F.K. ♥
Syrian Diplomat, Minister, Writer & Grandfather

The moment
I can put you
in a poem
is the moment
I know it's over.

I look forward
to seeing you
in a poem, caged
within four sides
of a page.
Between lines
and outside of me.
Your worth
inched out
into the margins.
Where you kept me
this whole time.

Death Wish

I have this fear,
after seeing man after man after man
berate an ambitious woman
for being one—
while simultaneously being his—
I'll never be able to believe
in the existence of a man
who can recognize
the honorable wealth
of this amalgamation.
But that's not the fear.
The fear is that this in turn
will subconsciously cause me
to restrict myself.
To walk on eggshells
in self-made shackles.
To stay on the safe side,
for the sake of love and loyalty.
Screw my deep-rooted loyalty,
it's brought me nothing but ache.

I fear
even when he tells me to go,
I'll stay.
I won't soar.
I'll chain myself down,
fly at low heights,
to please his fragile ego.
I saw other women do it
and they were safe.
Their men stayed—
not lovingly, but they stayed.
Like possessors,
proud owners of obedient pets.
Following nonverbal commands
on cue—unwritten rules.
I saw other women soar.

Break free of those chains
Extend their wings beautifully
across the horizons—East to West.
But their men, and their people,
poisoned their skies.
So all at once, flying
became both their life and their death.
And I'm here, left to decide,
which way do I want to die?

Demons

Have you ever thought that maybe
those inner demons
are just shadows
of your imagination?
Alive only
from the absence of light?
Their breath of life coming
from your refusal to let love in?
Flickering from the wilting candle
right in front of you?
Don't you have love to burn?
Ignite, and let both ends of this love burn
till we meet halfway.

Those were the words I ached
to tell him before I realized
he had no inner demons.
He *was* the demon.

Stepping Stones

I didn't love him
and I don't think he loved me either.
I just finished his story.
Fit in between all his blank spaces
but unevenly.
He didn't care.
I felt better than emptiness to him.
And maybe that's why I work well
with everyone.
I fill in their emptiness
they won't fill themselves.
That means they only ever need me.

But just because they *need* you
doesn't mean they *want* you.

Sunrise Cravings

Why are sunsets romanticized
if they signify the end?
We celebrate births of humanity,
grieve their ends.
What makes the sky any different?
Is it just our nature to glorify darkness above light?

I wanted to leave him
while he was sleeping.
Not because I didn't love him anymore
but because I could no longer wait
for him to decide whether or not
I was worth loving.

I'm   still   here
even though he left.

My first crush taught me Lesson 1:
*Just because you love someone
doesn't mean they will love you back.*

Age 16. Lesson 2:
A man's devotional obsession is not love.
He will wear it well anyway.
Spiritual men sing hymns of God
in their "love" for you.
Make you want to have faith,
want to worship harder.
But bruised knees showed me prayer
can't heal man—only me.

Age 20. Lesson 3:
This is what Love feels like.

Age 24. Lesson 4:
Love shouldn't hurt
but it's the weapon of choice in every battle.
Your white flags will be drenched in blood
and you still won't see them as red.
Surrender, this is not a war you can win.

Age 27. Lesson 5:
Love does not ask for your body as a prerequisite.
But when your body is taken advantage of
it no longer feels like yours.
And for a long time it doesn't.
For a long time it doesn't
feel   like   anything.

Give your spirit to God, scriptures plead,
then find your body healed.
But I am notorious for doing things in reverse.
And my body,
my body has tired of being taken by man.
So here, I give it to God instead and pray
that my spirit is healed in the process too.

Age 29. Lesson 6:
Men can only love me in pieces.
I was not created to be loved w h o l e.
Men love my body, not what I do with it.
Love that I am an artist, not the art I create.
Love my intellect,
but fear my thoughts *expressed*.
Love my activism, not the causes I fight for.
And I, I don't know how to love men
except whole.

Age Unknown. Lesson Yet to Be Learned:
*It's **their** loss.*
One day I'll believe that lie.
The one that resurrects every time another man leaves.
After all, God keeps sending me the flight risks—
perfect men to teach me—
but I keep learning a different lesson:
I am never enough.

Sometimes, the truths behind beautiful sunsets
aren't all that beautiful.
Somehow, we love them anyway.
I am that setting sun,
men, my purple skies.

Independence Day

If you won't commit to me,
then commit to staying away from me.

Empty Spaces

I sleep on the other side of my own bed
to give your ghost his

                    space.

His haunting means pain
and pain means feeling you

and if that's all I'll ever get, I'll take it.
Feeling pain to feel you

feels safer than feeling
your absence.

But do you miss me
with as much ache as I miss you?

Do you miss me
when I'm not there?

Pregnant Minds

Nine long agonizing months, watching
this demon of his grow
inside me. This life-altering
state of mind born
from the touch of a stranger
I thought I knew
as a friend, as a lover, as a man.
No surprise getting pregnant
after a one-night mind f***.
Wait, I don't curse, I mean I do,
but not like this. Not on the account
of someone so unworthy
of my time, my energy, my body.

I've been carrying this weight
of him, for him, and nothing
to justify doing so—no reasoning or rationale.
But tonight I felt the ghost
of that pressure between my thighs;
the bittersweet finale long overdue.
I gave birth to the truth
implanted somewhere inside me.
The irony of reproduction—
you give something that takes.

He was done with me after the first night
even though I never finished, but he burns
through women like he burns
through those cigarettes,
idly sitting in his front pocket.

I hope he burns
through every woman, one by one.
Unknowingly sets fire to an army of us.
Flames roaring louder than the shot
heard around the world.
Setting in motion a revolution.
Impregnating us with the ugly truth

we use to regrow the parts of us he destroyed.
Then I won't be alone, forced into silence
about what he's done—what he does—
pitying his way into the pants of plenty.
Making us believe our years
of friendship, our closeness and trust,
were nothing more than a false result
on a pregnancy test. The one we found
ourselves taking when our periods didn't come.

He asked me that night if I had come.
Yeah, I did, I had come to my goddamn senses.

1. Sleeping with him was not all the hype
he had made it out to be.
Mediocre at most, mind un-blown.

2. He didn't have as much game
in the bedroom as he did outside of it.

3. I had been strung along for *this*?

Oh f***, no wait, I don't curse,
I mean I do, but not like this.
Not for someone who saw me as nothing
more than just another cigarette in a box.
A woman of ashes between his fingers.

He said my substance and intelligence
make me distinct for fucking.
I say my substance and intelligence
make me distinct for loving.

But who knew dicks
had such high standards?

Graduation Day

Boys will never shirk from needing me.
Unknowingly, I am the eternal supply
to their unhealthy demand.
Feeding them truths their mothers never did.
Truths mothers refused to feed them
for fear they'd grow into the same men
they married, or fear they wouldn't.
So the cycle repeats,
and I find myself holding a boy
the size of a man.
Educating him all over again
on how to be human.
How to love a woman
whole, without breaking her.
A woman is not to be loved in pieces,
yet I am always broken in the process.
Only ever knowing how to teach hands on.
Learning by example means my love
becomes the visual aid they need
to finally graduate into men
for someone else.

Writings on the Wall

He says he knows
his way around a woman,
yet here I am
dancing circles around him.

I look at his past,
the collection of women
he's entertained—all a certain type.
Micro-relationships, he calls them.
One matching category,
and I, the outlier.

It must be my exoticism that calls him—
not exotic by ethnicity,
exotic by personality.
I know he's not lying when he says
I am not like the others.
Even if we tried,
I couldn't fit the lineup.
But how long will this foreignness of mine
keep him around?

Soundproof Mouths

I keep looking for the woman
I used to be *before*.

Before him.
                    Before him.
                                        Before him.

I cannot find her but
I'm not sure I even want to
anymore.

Is it consensual
if his skin can't be found
under my fingernails?
If the remnants of the woman
I used to be
are beneath his?

Men tell me
my resilience draws them.
My ability to survive trauma.
But their addiction
is only to the conquest.
Attracted to the exoticism
of a broken strong woman.

Is it consensual
if my no was inaudible?
Entangled somewhere
between twisted vocal cords
and soundproof mouths?

Is it consensual
if my yes was merely three letters
strung together like pearls?
A noose he tied around my neck.
So delicately, so dark,
I couldn't see I was conflating fear with love.

R.I.P.
Every forced laugh I ever conceived
when I confused frightened with flirting.

R.I.P.
Every dress I ever bought
to wear for a man
instead of myself.

R.I.P.
To the woman I once was,
whoever she once was.
May she rest in peace.
Better yet, pieces.

Taste of Words

Remember when you read your poetry to him?

    He never tasted the same after that.

Like your words refined your taste

    to accept only the finer people who never left you,

who never left you

    with a bitter taste in your mouth.

Tongue Twister

My tongue had struggled
to wrap itself
in pronunciation of you.
But after you left,
your name
was the only language
it could speak.

The End

You were nothing more
than a climactic scene
to one chapter of my story,
because we've achieved
no happily ever after,
nor were you the end of me.

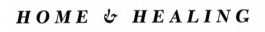

HOME & HEALING

New Pieces

The world puts you to the test.
Strives to break you.
You can keep fighting against it
or you can finally let it win.
Choose the latter.
Collapse.
Sure, you lose
fragments of yourself,
but you learn what is meant
by less is more.
Shattering into pieces
sharpens your edges.
Creates jagged redevelopments.
Thicker skin.
Exile from fitting in—
for good.
Give in.
Let the world break you,
but this time around,
make sure you are the one
who rebuilds yourself.

Fall

Maybe when the trees start to shed
I too can shake my heavy trunk,
find that survivor, trapped
somewhere beneath the fallen leaves.

Me (Part Duex)

I wish I knew
the *me* I'd become
after you, but I guess
you had to break me first.
How else was I to come
out of my shell?
Rise up from the ashes
of who I thought
I'd be forever?
I loved her so much.
This new woman, though,
I don't know.
She's taught me a lot already—
like where my real lines are
and how much easier
it is to cross them.

I'm learning who I am
all over again.
I wonder how long
it'll take me to love her
this time around.

Apple

Teta, my maternal grandmother,
sugarcoats the cracks on the banana colored walls

of the home that once used to be minty green,
as resulting from old age and not war.

The sun warms her back, as she plays solitaire
on the iPhone she unwrapped a week before.

On the quiet afternoons, when even the bombs retire,
we spend the hours talking tech.

I teach her how to upload photos, reset passwords,
download apps—like solitaire—

and how to send audio messages.
Your next lesson will be teaching me how to see you

on this, she says,
so that we can talk when you go back home.

"خلص إن شاء الله بكرا تيتة."
Tomorrow, I tell her,

vividly remembering her daughter,
over seven thousand miles away.

The way she too asks me to teach her tech.
How to share a link on Facebook,

the difference between a post and a story,
and how to unfreeze her phone.

I guess the apple really doesn't fall far from the tree,
not even when one is in Syria, and the other, America.

Ajnabeeyeh

I say I am homesick,
but I wonder,
am I just sick of these places
they tell me are supposed to be home?
Or sick of these people
who never make me feel at home?

Generous Servings

I know how it feels to be looked at like a feast
overdone—too much. A colorfully vast table spread
unfolding in infinitely exotic flavors men want to devour:
spicy Aleppine red peppers,
sweetly sugared bitter orange rinds,
tangy pomegranate molasses.
Seasonings still surviving ages of colonization.
Lying atop a hand stitched and gold-freckled
powder blue Damascene tablecloth.

What a difference it is though to be seen
as a table of too much food
with gratitude—for the coming leftovers—
versus a table of burdens.
Excess clutter of heavy glass Tupperware, stacked.
Foreign foods rotting in a familiar fridge.

I pack up the scraps of my mismatched identity,
like clashing sets of different china—
extra place settings rolled out for picky guests—
and I question, when I am told I am too much,
how exactly am I so?

Am I too much like the weight
on the full belly behind the shirt button,
ready to burst at the table?
Too much like the cologne that walks into the dinner party
way before the man does?

The unnecessary housewarming gift
that becomes a favor you must return.
A never-ending exchange of debts our children inherit.
The misshapen thickness of a blue-based
black eyeliner or the blush on an '80s cheek?

Too much like the bubbling water spilling
out from beneath the lid of a pot cooking lentils?

I must be too much,
like that fire beneath the boiling pot.

Doubling the volume of water's ever evolving form.
Like the thick white envelope of cash my grandparents
would gift me on those summer trips to Syria.
Thousands and thousands of Syrian pounds
between my American fingers.
Spend it wisely, they would say,
having known the flavor of poverty
and praying their grandchildren never taste it.

My palette still reminisces over the fruits of Shaalan.
The cute guy at the *Ya Hala* smoothie kiosk
who'd tell me I gave him too much money,
until I finally learned the language of my other home's currency.
I think I am too much,

like that extra inch on the pastel pink ribbons
mama cuts and curls for the many colorful balloons
she'd flood our room with every last day of Ramadan.
The marble cake she'd bake two days in a row
for the sweet teeth of her three children.
What a feast she'd create—
too much magic for such little souls, and yet it fit,
like neatly piled Tupperware of blessings.
Bites of home awaiting us after long days at school.

Mama's lineage taught us how to be too much.
How beautiful love blooms from its buds.
Its spillage being an attribute of Arab generosity—
timeless and transcending, no matter where we call home.
No matter what table we sit at.

Too much, is the least we can do.

Origami Home

Pangea is an immigrant's bedtime story;
the Damask rose fairytales she inhales,
and where home / and home
have no ocean between them.

A paper lantern globe flattened / accordion style /
into heart lines of familiarly foreign palms;
cutting corners, creating edges
on an earth too round.

Flat surfaces have ends, have final destinations,
have everyone / gathering / close / sacrificing
blood—from once proud fingers—
to sew home back together again.

Familiar Face

i.

Teta calls me to her room,
a request usually accompanied with a gift.
Sometimes a Kit Kat bar from her secret stash,
other times 5,000 Syrian Pounds rolled in her palm.
She points to an aged ivory album on her bed.
Want to see your grandfather and I's wedding photos?

ii.

Mama and I sit at the dining table, snacking
on cheese, chocolate, and bread—the way we used to
at Teta and Jiddo's house during early mornings in Syria.
She keeps looking at me, as if catching glimpses
of someone familiar from long ago.

iii.

Do you notice how I'm not wearing any makeup? Teta asks
as we softly turn pages of black and white memories.
In a simple white dress and a matching headband,
she stands beside my handsome grandfather—
her signature minimalist smile gracing a naked face—
and I am mesmerized by the perfection of her beauty.

iv.

I ramble on to mama between bites of cheese,
her expression still swinging between confusion and familiarity.
Our eyes interlock and she asks, *You're not wearing makeup
today are you?* I shake my head and she says,
You look so beautiful, like your teta.

Selfie

They say selfies
are a sign of narcissism
but that's okay.
It's about time I learned
how to face myself
and what self-love really is.

The Remodel

They say if it ain't broke, don't fix it.
But what if it's semi broken?
A kitchen of 23 years calls for help.
It never asked to be uprooted.
Demoted from a home to a house.
Remodeled into what the modern times call *innovative*.
We lost our space
in what used to be our central space.
We lost our mother's kitchen.
The collective nook that collected us,
with its rose blush wood and Damascene cuisines
Thursdays after school.
Glass dishes, hand painted
with royal blue European designs
that called to her childhood.
Scratched up cutting boards
that defied 21st century cutting-edge designs.
They were right when they said,
they don't make 'em like they used to.
Nothing fits anymore—
not our Tupperware nor our spirits.
We feel suffocated in the dark kitchen that lacks luster,
despite its lustrous stainless steel.
It doesn't resonate of the same Arabian touch
that birthed home
to our Syrian migration.
Its bland matte walls echo a silence
that once used to be bilingual chaos.
If walls could talk...
yet familiar aromas always lure us back into that space.

The basil sits at the corner
of our state-of-the-art marble counter top,
withering in a reminder of us.
My mother's favorite herb that she said
always tastes better when fresh.
Rich dirt holding it from its roots, taunting
us of the roots our kitchen once had.

She slices the peppers differently now.
Her hands nostalgic for the enthusiasm
that once came with our pink kitchen.
Now they grasp at the surface of an umber one,
as foreign as she once was to this country.
As foreign as I'm beginning to feel
in this country, where my roots were planted.

Party of One

Her hands became mine / Calling everyone to the table / But everyone was only me / Not even she / I honored her / As best a second generation immigrant daughter could / More American than Syrian / at times / At times when fries substitute falafel / Shrimp / okra / And square white bread / for round speckled pita / The only thing connecting me back to my ancestors / was the prayer I made beforehand / in the Arabic tongue / about to taste dinner / in another language

Mother Tongue

The letters 'P' and 'V' do not exist in Arabic
yet over time, colloquialism drove it to yield.
Brought a language to its knees,

contorted its exotic tongue to say words
its origins never birthed.
Why is it then, when a language is forced to bow

in prostration to a colonizer's demand,
you, oh child of the language, stiffen your tongue
in obedience to their foreign dialect and break

your name—instead of bread—to make peace?
Names are loud embodiments of our culture.
Deserving to be spoken in volumes—

waves of sound beating drums in our ears.
Awakening the histories of our ancestors buried
beneath the dirt and blood of stolen lands.

Never let your name roll off your tongue, diluted
to ease its pronunciation for others. Say it
as it was meant to be said. Say it

the way your immigrant father and refugee mother
said it while you still nestled tightly in the womb.
Simmering sweetly inside the core, still uncut

from your roots. Names are beautiful
in their complexities. Worthy of being planted
in mouths, in between the spaces of teeth.

They are meant to be stumbled on, meant to take time.
Untie that knotted flesh and speak your mother tongue
proudly. Let the curves of each letter cradle and nurture

every tradition broken in the breakage of names.
Enunciate every corner of your darkened words.
Tongues are marvelously flexible creatures.

Residual

Dialects: Varying fonts
of tongues calligraphing prayer—
in double helix—on Arabic

skin. Fair.
Unfair, as in property.
Mine?

Tattoos: Haram.
A prohibition of darkening
snow with blood

words.
Of body autonomy.
Mine.

Name: Mispronounced
but only in America, only if immigrant,
only every generation, even after

twenty-nine: Years of hearing everything
except my name.
It trips on the shoelaces of foreign

tongues. Tastes languages
like the licking of envelopes
shut. Sealing away

residual bitterness,
but only for the throat
holding it hostage.

How do I wear the skin of an Arab writer / with Arabs
after years of being
an Arab writer / with Americans?

Skin
does
shed.

Based on a True Story

The sense of smell is the strongest
associated with memory,
but what about sound?
A scary movie on mute
is not scary anymore.
So what does Syria sound like?
I can't hear it—
not how I used to anyway.
Syria had magic and magic has a sound:
6 a.m. serenity on Saturday mornings—
no cars in the street.
Birds, nature's alarm clock.
Magic sounds like my grandparents
shuffling to their daily cup of coffee.
Like soft whispers
before the rest of the city awakens.
A vendor winding chains to open up shop.
Blasting scriptures on audio systems,
asking God to bless his earnings for the day.
Magic sounds like busy market streets.
Men yelling and whistling from one kiosk to another
for something, for everything.
Magic sounds like children laughing.
Kicking neon soccer balls in between alleyways.
Like cars honking.
Traffic.
Smog.
Arabic.
Magic sounds like Arabic
kissing the walls of Damascene neighborhoods.
Like history, still alive today.
Its heartbeat so loud, so loud.
Pulsating in the secret pathways
that speak stories people don't yet know of.
Magic sounds like poetry.
Words flowing of proverbs that never get old.
Magic sounds like your neighbors checking in on you.
You checking in on them.
It never being a burden

but a duty of pleasure.
Solidarity.
Magic sounds like never asking what their religion is.
What their political background is.
Magic sounds like peace.

Syria doesn't sound like this anymore.
Or maybe it's gone silent,
after the world grew deaf to its screams,
because Syria sounds like terror now
and terror has a sound.
It sounds like a mother
divvying up how to save only two of her six children
because that's how many hands she has.
Like a father's kiss on the cheek
of another corpse called son.
Terror sounds like low-flying jets.
Whistling shells soaring over in arches.
Red is the only color left on the Syrian rainbow.
Terror sounds like politicians becoming the many cooks
who spoiled the broth.
Syria is the broth.
Terror sounds like nine years passing in silence.
Like a child crying.
Begging to go to school.
Begging to know that they can sleep
and wake up the next day.
Terror sounds like peace and ceasefire
are the two biggest lies.
Like my grandfather counting down to death, aloud.
My grandmother crying more than I've ever remembered.
And terror sounds like a refugee dying
to live.
And unlike the scary movie,
Syria is not based on a true story,
it *is* the true story
and you can't mute the truth.

So can you hear Syria?
Are you listening?

Body & Soul

الحروب تقتل الناس
و حروب القلوب تقتل النفوس
و الألم
واحد

Wars kill people
and wars of the hearts kill souls.
And the pain
is one.

Parent Plant

If, after the storm,
I have lost a few petals
but I am still here,
praise yourself,

mama; the seeds you planted
birthed a moon flower.
Her roots growing
deeper than the hyphen
between Muslim-American.
Grounded to her origins,
yet reaching up
to a third culture
in her cross-pollinated bloom.

tiny plant

A weed is any plant that's growing where you don't want it. Some weeds are ugly. Some are pretty. But nearly all share the nasty habit of growing out of control, coming up everywhere, and making you want to shut yourself in a dark room.

—Steve Bender

Weed is feminine in Arabic,
'ishbeh daarra—a vicious herb,
nicknamed harshly
for her hopeful habit to grow.
Man calls her ugly, nasty,
unwanted, out of control.

Why does man hate what grows
independent; what learns to thrive
despite poison to its roots?
Our world teaches us to cut more
than to sew, to fear
what keeps on living,
even after death.
Like the earth, after rain
seeps through its parched skin.
Like a weed, after man paved
roads above her home.

At seven, I remember, mama
pointing a ginger pink finger
to the wet pavement; her smile, divine.
Overlooking the contrasting short greens,
Look, she says, with God so loudly
on her breath, *Subhanallah,*
look how this tiny plant
has just enough strength to break even
the thickest concrete
man needs hammers to crack through.

Mama's vision is resilience, her eyes
seeing beauty in everything,
specifically the overlooked.
Seeing the hope entangled
between the arms of weeds,
outstretched at the marvel of survival.

Of rebellion, of woman's nature.
How do hands defile what teaches bodies
persistence?
The manifestation of rebirth and relentlessness.
What plants hope beneath our soles
but still stays soft
in the process of breakthroughs.

Life After Death

Based off scripture, mama doesn't call it rain,
she calls it water. Watches it drip down

windows and cheeks. Sending us messages—
nature's Morse code—

tapping on the earth. Soil secrets.
I hear it. So much grace.

A lullaby to sleep, to live.
God tells us about life after death

but He shows us like this—in a superbloom.
Lets us taste it with kisses from these buds;

blossoming after the spill of water
on their lifeless threads.

Acknowledgements

Thank you to the following publications where these poems have previously appeared, sometimes in a different form:

"Apple" – *Like Home* by accoutrements: a public literary series project (2019)

"Chimera" – *Spillway 27* by Tebot Bach (2019)

"tiny plant" – *StoryLine Magazine* by Coastline Community Colleges (2019)

About the Author

Dania Ayah Alkhouli (a.k.a. Lady Narrator) is a Syrian writer, blogger, poet, editor, and author, born and raised in Southern California. Alkhouli earned her B.A. in Sociology and her M.A. in Public Policy & Administration from California State University, Long Beach. She published her debut book at 19, titled *91 at 19*. In 2017 she released her second poetry book, *Oceans & Flames*, a collection of poetry shedding light on her experience with, and survival of, domestic violence. Her work has also been featured in a few anthologies including, *The Silent Journey*, *Seven Countries*, and the *V Poetry Anthology*.

Alkhouli's work centers on feminism, mental health, sexuality, identity, culture, religion, and more recently on her war-torn homeland, Syria, and on grief, loss, and death. She has been featured on *Buzzfeed* and *Jubilee Media*, and has performed across national venues such as Da Poetry Lounge in Los Angeles, House Slam in Boston, and Busboys & Poets in D.C.

In 2012, Alkhouli and her mother founded the nonprofit organization, *A Country Called Syria*, a traveling exhibition showcasing the history and culture of their country. Their goal is to tour the exhibit nationwide and eventually establish a permanent base in SoCal where the community can connect even more deeply with Syria and its rich heritage. This will include the launch of their project to collect and archive the oral histories of locally resettled Syrian refugees in Southern California.

Patrons

Moon Tide Press would like to thank the following people for their support in helping publish the finest poetry from the Southern California region. To sign up as a patron, visit www.moontidepress.com or send an email to publisher@moontidepress.com.

Anonymous
Robin Axworthy
Conner Brenner
Bill Cushing
Susan Davis
Peggy Dobreer
Dennis Gowans
Alexis Rhone Fancher
Half Off Books & Brad T. Cox
Jim & Vicky Hoggatt
Michael Kramer
Ron Koertge & Bianca Richards
Ray & Christi Lacoste
Zachary & Tammy Locklin
Lincoln McElwee
David McIntire
José Enrique Medina
Andrew November
Michael Miller & Rachanee Srisavasdi
Michelle & Robert Miller
Terri Niccum
Ronny & Richard Morago
Jennifer Smith
Andrew Turner
Mariano Zaro

Also Available from
Moon Tide Press

The only thing that makes sense is to grow, Scott Ferry (2020)
Dead Letter Box, Terri Niccum (2019)
Tea and Subtitles: Selected Poems 1999-2019, Michael Miller (2019)
At the Table of the Unknown, Alexandra Umlas (2019)
The Book of Rabbits, Vince Trimboli (2019)
Everything I Write Is a Love Song to the World, David McIntire (2019)
Letters to the Leader, HanaLena Fennel (2019)
Darwin's Garden, Lee Rossi (2019)
Dark Ink: A Poetry Anthology Inspired by Horror (2018)
Drop and Dazzle, Peggy Dobreer (2018)
Junkie Wife, Alexis Rhone Fancher (2018)
The Moon, My Lover, My Mother, & the Dog, Daniel McGinn (2018)
Lullaby of Teeth: An Anthology of Southern California Poetry (2017)
Angels in Seven, Michael Miller (2016)
A Likely Story, Robbi Nester (2014)
Embers on the Stairs, Ruth Bavetta (2014)
The Green of Sunset, John Brantingham (2013)
The Savagery of Bone, Timothy Matthew Perez (2013)
The Silence of Doorways, Sharon Venezio (2013)
Cosmos: An Anthology of Southern California Poetry (2012)
Straws and Shadows, Irena Praitis (2012)
In the Lake of Your Bones, Peggy Dobreer (2012)
I Was Building Up to Something, Susan Davis (2011)
Hopeless Cases, Michael Kramer (2011)
One World, Gail Newman (2011)
What We Ache For, Eric Morago (2010)
Now and Then, Lee Mallory (2009)
Pop Art: An Anthology of Southern California Poetry (2009)
In the Heaven of Never Before, Carine Topal (2008)
A Wild Region, Kate Buckley (2008)
Carving in Bone: An Anthology of Orange County Poetry (2007)
Kindness from a Dark God, Ben Trigg (2007)
A Thin Strand of Lights, Ricki Mandeville (2006)
Sleepyhead Assassins, Mindy Nettifee (2006)
Tide Pools: An Anthology of Orange County Poetry (2006)
Lost American Nights: Lyrics & Poems, Michael Ubaldini (2006)

Made in the USA
San Bernardino, CA
09 February 2020